Papa's Place

MARGARET JENSEN

Here's Life Publishers

Published by
HERE'S LIFE PUBLISHERS, INC.
P.O. Box 1576
San Bernardino, California 92402

Library of Congress Cataloging-in-Publication Data
Jensen, Margaret T. (Margaret Tweten), 1916-

    Papa's Place
1. Tweten, Elius N., d. 1973.   2. Baptists — Clergy — Biography.
3. Jensen, Margaret T. (Margaret Tweten), 1916-   .   I. Title
BX6495.T8J46   1987   286'.13   [B]   87-12
ISBN 0-89840-175-5 (pbk.)

HLP Product No. 951731
© 1987, Margaret Tweten Jensen

Scripture references are from the King James Version of the Bible.

FOR MORE INFORMATION WRITE:

L.I.F.E. — P.O. Box A399, Sydney South 2000, Australia
Campus Crusade for Christ of Canada — Box 300, Vancouver, B.C., V6C 2X3, Canada
Campus Crusade for Christ — Pearl Assurance House, 4 Temple Row, Birmingham, B2 5HG, England
Campus Crusade for Christ — P.O. Box 240, Colombo Court Post Office, Singapore 9117
Lay Institute for Evangelism — P.O. Box 8786, Auckland 3, New Zealand
Great Commission Movement of Nigeria — P.O. Box 500, Jos, Plateau State Nigeria, West Africa
Campus Crusade for Christ International — Arrowhead Springs, San Bernardino, CA 92414, U.S.A.

DEDICATED TO PAPA'S CHILDREN
The Grandchildren

MARGARET'S CHILDREN:
Janice Jensen Carlberg
Daniel Jensen
Ralph Jensen

GORDON'S CHILDREN:
Ray Tweten
Nancy Tweten Fjordbatten
Don Tweten
Kurt Tweten

DORIS'S CHILDREN:
Doreen Hammer Mabe
Donald Hammer
Davidson Hammer
Duane Hammer

JOYCE SOLVEIG'S CHILDREN:
Judy Jensen Marschewski
Paul Jensen
Steve Jensen

JEANELLE'S CHILDREN:
Robert Keiter
Charlene Keiter Strand

CONTENTS

CONTENTS

Sing, O heavens;
and be joyful, O earth;
and break forth into singing, O mountains:
for the Lord hath comforted his people,
and will have mercy upon his afflicted.

(Isaiah 49:13)

And when ye stand praying,
forgive,
if ye have ought against any:
that your Father also
which is in heaven
may forgive you your trespasses.

(Mark 11:25)

SPECIAL THANKS

To Leslie H. Stobbe and all the staff of Here's Life Publishers Inc., for being a special kind of family.

To Jim Warren, host of *Prime Time America,* for his encouragement to the "Story Teller."

To all my new friends in America, Canada, and Scandinavia for their warm letters and calls that inspire me to keep telling the old, old story of Jesus and His love.

To Harold: Words aren't enough to thank my husband of forty-nine years for his constant support and for working and traveling with me, side by side.

We both thank our daughter, Janice, for being the most precious daughter anyone could have and also for being our best friend and our travel agent.

Her husband, Dr. R. Judson Carlberg, our favorite son-in-law, is also my number 1 fan!

"Thank you" to my six grandchildren who keep me "young in heart."

I want to thank the readers of this book for bearing patiently with me as we go back and forth into times and places. I believe God has a special message for each one of us as we listen to the still, small voice of the Great Communicator.

God bless you all!

INTRODUCTION

The Episcopal rector and I sat together watching the people fill the fellowship hall for a church banquet.

Tonight I would be sharing stories from my book, *First We Have Coffee,* a book about Mama and her coffee pot — but more than that, a book about God's faithfulness through a special child of His. Laughter and tears flow through the pages.

"I loved your book, Margaret," the priest whispered to me, "but your mother was an angel." He shrugged offhandedly. "Who can identify with her? Why don't you write about Papa? He sounds like quite a character — and someone with whom we mortals can relate."

We laughed together; then the meeting began.

Some months later, our daughter, Janice, suggested the title, "Papa's Place." Papa called Janice his "princess," and she loved him.

Still I hesitated.

Did I really want to tell Papa's story? I wanted my children and my grandchildren to know that Papa was a godly man. But did I want them to know that this strong, sturdy Norwegian, who had been loved by so many was given to anger, and could explode easily? Even more, did I want to admit the pain, the hurt that I often had felt as a child, or that at times I actually had feared my father?

Did I want to portray both sides of my beloved Papa, to tarnish his pastoral image with my own raw memories of his one prevailing flaw? I looked at my daughter Janice and then across the room to her children, my grandchildren.

Yes, my children and my grandchildren had a right to know Papa Tweten as he was, the fallible, flesh-and-blood man I knew and loved. He was part of their roots — the branch from which they sprang. There was joy in telling Mama's story — she was so loving, so caring, so full of faith. But both Mama and Papa were part of my children's heritage.

Mama and Papa! Mama was like a flowing river, blessing the banks of life around her. Papa was like a mountain stream rushing through rocks and brush to reach the river. He knew his source — God. But he found his rightful place when the restless stream met the river — Mama.

Now I was going back to a long-ago time. I was remembering Papa. . .

1

The Journey

MAMA PACKED A BOX with clean clothes, carefully folded, so as not to wrinkle my starched dresses and petticoats. Two were for everyday; one was for Sunday. Papa's white shirt lay on top. Then she picked up the box and I followed her outside where Papa was cranking up the old Model-T Ford with its thin tires and snap-on curtains. With a quick smile, he kissed Mama, Grace, Gordon and Doris good-bye. As Mama held me tightly, the lump in my throat grew bigger. My younger sisters and brother lined up to kiss me and stood in awe of this astonishing occasion.

I was going with Papa on a missionary journey!

We were leaving our home at 510 Avenue J, Saskatoon, Saskatchewan, to drive on the open roads through the Canadian prairie. As we pulled away that bright summer day in 1928, I waved until the four-room white-trimmed yellow house, with the outhouse in back, faded into the distance. In my mind I could see Mama putting on the coffee pot and the children dipping their sugar lump in Mama's coffee.

Papa and I drove over the dusty roads in silence. Communicating with his children was not Papa's place. It was up to God and Mama to bring up Mama's children. He had the Lord's work to do. Papa taught theology; Mama taught the living.

I didn't need to talk. It was enough to know that Papa told Mama he needed me. Papa wanted me along? This was history in the making! I didn't think he needed anyone, but I heard him tell Mama just before driving away, "The journey is long and Margaret is good company. Besides, she can play the organ in the tent meetings."

As the old black Ford rattled over the ruts in the road, I sat prim and proper with my hands folded in my lap — a scrawny twelve-year-old with bobbed blond hair and blue eyes almost as bright and clear as Papa's. A plain full skirt stretched over my starched petticoat, partially hiding my gangly legs.

Unaware of me, Papa sang the old hymns in his clear tenor and practiced his Norwegian sermons in English since he preached in both languages.

I clutched my clean handkerchief and sat up straight. This was a moment to remember. Once or twice I stole a glance his way. I was in awe of my handsome father in his black suit and high starched collar. Papa was a clean-shaven man with a full face and high forehead and bushy blond eyebrows that overshadowed his piercing blue eyes. He was slender, barely six feet on tiptoe, but to me he was tall, a tower of strength.

I tried to remember Mama's instructions. "Keep Papa's clothes clean and be sure he has the starched white shirt for Sunday meeting." Mama had hugged me again and whispered, "I'll miss you, Margaret, and I'll miss you helping with the children." The lump in my throat came back.

From the open window of the car I watched the rolling fields of Saskatchewan and the isolated farmlands of the Norwegian immigrants. Towering pines stretched toward the sky. White clouds floated lazily in the blue expanse above us. The wind on the prairie sang a song of its own. But Papa was oblivious of me and of the splash of sun on the miles of grain waving in the summer wind. I relaxed, breathing deep — loving the earthen smell of wheat fields and barnyards.

When we came to the first farm, the children waved and the cattle stared at us with big brown eyes. Kittens and chickens scurried in the garden. The horses plodded along, pulling the plow. They tugged at their restraints as the chugging, spouting Model-T roared down the lane, disrupting the quiet countryside.

The farmer's wife wiped her hands on her apron and offered us a drink of cold water or a cup of coffee. Papa and the farmer exchanged news and finally Papa extended an invitation to the tent meeting.

The children and I looked shyly at each other, then talked about kittens and things.

After a prayer for God's blessing on the farmer's family, Papa cranked up the Ford and we continued on our way.

"Ja, Margaret, we stay at the Thompson's house this time, and you will help Mrs. Thompson with the chores and housework. Deacon Salen's daughter Cora plays the organ at the tent meeting, but if she can't come, then you will play the hymns you have learned."

I promised to help Mrs. Thompson and play the organ. No one argued with Papa! We drifted back into silence. I was remembering another time on another farm — when I helped. I shuddered. That was the time Uncle Barney rescued Grace and me from our farm "vacation" where we scrubbed floors, rubbed clothes on a wash board and ironed with irons heated on the wood stove. We weeded the garden, gathered eggs and cleaned the separator after the milking. At night Grace and I crawled into bed, clinging to each other in utter despair and homesickness. We vowed never to leave Mama again!

This was different. Papa needed me! That was enough!

Mama was like a harbor, safe and secure, like a river deep and flowing. Papa was like a restless sea, with sudden flashes of temper like a summer storm. Then, as suddenly, Papa's songs and laughter came back, like sunshine after rain. When the storms came we ran to Mama who explained that Papa never understood children because he had never been a child.

Softly she would remind us, "Papa's parents died when he was very young. He never had a real childhood." She would hug us and add, "When he was seventeen years old he came to America to study." Perhaps Papa didn't understand children, but Mama said that he understood loneliness and fear.

It seemed that Mama understood everything — most of all Papa. She loved him.

The waving fields swept by while Papa sang old Norwegian songs. I was remembering another time, when I was six years old, a long time ago. It was the time Papa threw the rag doll, Big Jack, into the furnace.

I wept for my well-worn rag doll — my only one. But Papa thought it was part of the debris he swept up in the Winnipeg parsonage basement. Always in a hurry, he shoveled the contents into the furnace.

It was then that Mama explained, "Papa never had a toy and doesn't understand the ways of a rag doll and a six-year-old girl." She wiped my tears. "Besides, I will make a new rag doll for you. You must forgive Papa." I tried to forget about the rag doll, but I always remembered the little boy who didn't have a toy.

I stole another glance at Papa sitting up straight and tall, his broad hands on the steering wheel. He turned to me with a chuckle. "Ja, Margaret, so what do you think, going with your Papa on a missionary journey — like Paul and Timothy?" He laughed with abandoned joy and sang "Standing on the Promises." He loved the freedom of the open road and his Model-T. And he loved the journey he was taking. This was Papa's parish — the scattered, Scandinavian immigrants of the province of Saskatchewan. The farmers lived miles apart, but that didn't bother Papa. "When I come they get together for meetings in the schoolhouse," he said, "or they pitch a tent in the summertime."

As though talking to himself he mused out loud, "The Scandinavian settlers are strong and full of faith. You'll see, Margaret. They learn to live with a new language, blizzards, even crop failures. But their greatest test is loneliness." His smile faded for a moment. "Some wait for years for their families to come from Europe. Some families never come. We are blessed, Margaret. We have Mama . . . there's no one like Mama." I turned. His blue eyes were on me. "The first time I saw your Mama I said, 'That is the wife for me!' " Papa chuckled delightedly. "I even forgot my sermon — but I married Mama three months later."

As we rode along, I forgot my awe of Papa and we talked about the time we came to Saskatchewan and lived in the chicken house. "Do you remember the chicken house, Papa?"

Papa's laughter rolled over the prairie as we remembered together. "The farmer? I see him now," Papa said. "I asked him for a house for my family to stay in."

"Ja, Ja," Papa said, mimicking the farmer. "Ve have a house for you for the summer. It vas our first home and I built it myself."

Behind the thorny bushes and scrub pine had stood a weather-beaten house hidden from view. When we reached it, I knew why it was hidden. Chickens flew in every direction cackling a loud protest over the eviction notice.

Mice scampered, but not for long. Flies were everywhere. We peeked through the broken windows and walked on the loose floor boards. Spiderwebs clung to the walls. The doors squeaked on rusty hinges.

We laughed now as we bumped and bounced on the high, hard seats of the Model-T. But we didn't laugh back then. Papa continued, "Ja, I remember the farmer said, 'Plenty of food in the storehouse, and my vimmen vill see that you get vot you need. Come, I'll show you the storehouse before I go back to the fields.' "

The farmer's beautiful house stood on the hill, surrounded by gardens of flowers and vegetables. Across the road were barns and storehouses bursting with the fruits of plentiful harvests. Cattle and horses grazed in the lush pastures. Hired men worked in the fields. In the barn were buggies and wagons and a shiny new car.

I sighed. "I remember the big house, Papa, when the farmer welcomed us all into a large spacious room with beautiful polished floors. The floor was waxed like glass and I was afraid to walk on it. The mother and daughters had a table spread for all of us and for the hired men. The whole house seemed full of sunshine."

"Ja," Papa agreed, "they were good cooks and had a big dinner for us."

I remembered the winding staircase leading to spacious bedrooms. Lace curtains blew in the breeze. *This had to be what heaven was like,* I thought, *beautiful sunlit rooms!*

But after the lovely meal, we said our polite, "Takk for maten" (thanks for the food), and headed for the chicken house.

Mama flew into perpetual motion. Scrub bucket, soap and brushes were passed around. Everyone scrubbed something. Fels Naphtha soap and Lysol did the job. Cardboard replaced broken windows and Papa nailed down the loose floor boards. Long strips of fly paper caught the flies and we learned to duck to avoid the sticky entanglement.

The Ford chugged along. Papa chuckled, "Mama even

had me scrubbing." He, too, was remembering.

Within hours the house was clean! The large room downstairs had a polished cookstove, a table and some chairs. The ladder to the loft revealed a large sleeping room with one bed. Mama hung a quilt-partition for privacy. Four pallets were laid on the newly scrubbed floor.

"Ja, ja, Margaret, the dinner in the big house was good. But when we had cleaned the chicken house, Mama put on the coffee pot. Now, let me tell you one thing: No one can cook like Mama — or make such good coffee."

I remembered the starched cloth on the old wooden table, and the wild flowers Grace picked and put in a glass jar. We all scrubbed up outside where Mama had a basin of water. A towel hung on a nail by the door. No dirt would enter Mama's clean kitchen. With our shoes off, we gathered around the table to give thanks. We were a family. We had a home. Papa even let us dip our sugar lumps in his coffee. All was well. Papa was in his place.

Even now I could hear the sound of that first night — wind over the prairie, mice scampering about, flies buzzing on the sticky fly paper and the lonely howl of a coyote.

"But Papa," I ventured now, "that farmer said his barn was full."

"Ja, but the wife had the key."

I had watched, bewildered, as the farmer's wife carefully counted the eggs and offered skimmed milk, a bowl of flour and a bowl of sugar. "They had so much, Papa, and gave so little — and you and Mama have so little and give so much."

"I know, Margaret, I know. It is all such a mystery," Papa said solemnly. "The poor heard Jesus gladly, and the poor give cheerfully. But always remember, Margaret, it is the spirit of giving that God blesses — and a thankful heart, like Mama says." He took one hand from the steering wheel and rubbed his chin thoughtfully. "Somehow God always takes care of us — ja, in spite of me, Mama says. I just give everything away. That is not always wisdom, but Mama knows I can't turn from anyone in need."

"Papa, do you remember the time Mama had the toothache?" We laughed together now. But back then I had cried.

It was a hot summer day and Papa was on one of his missionary journeys to visit farmers in other towns, a journey that sometimes took several days.

Mama's face was red and swollen with pain from an infected tooth. The farmer's shiny new car, with real glass windows (not like Papa's car with the snap-on curtains), stood in the barn beside the wagons and buggy.

Timidly Mama asked the farmer if someone could drive her to town to see the dentist but he shook his head. It was harvest time and crops had to be gathered. A tooth didn't seem too important. No help could be spared.

One of the hired men offered to hitch up the horse and buggy so Mama could drive to town, ten miles away. She gave me instructions to care for the children. As she gathered up every penny she had to buy a bag of flour, I protested, "But, Mama, the farmer's barns are full!"

"I know," Mama answered softly, "but the heart is empty." Somehow I understood.

I watched her wrap a scarf around her swollen face and clutch her money in a handkerchief. With a snap of the reins she was off. I went back into our "chicken coop" house and played games with the children, watching uneasily as storm clouds gathered in the sky.

It was almost dark when the horse and buggy pulled into the farm yard. The hired man unhitched the horses and sadly shook his head. Mama was soaked and the wet scarf clung to her face. She was crying as she said, "The dentist was gone and I was caught in a bad storm. My precious bag of flour is soaked!" In the house she crumpled into the rocking chair while we gathered around her and pulled off her wet shoes. Silently I prayed that God would help us to get flour for bread and get Mama's tooth fixed.

Then we heard the sputtering of Papa's car. We shouted for joy! Papa was furious — not at us, for a change, but at the circumstances. "Come, Mama, I know a good dentist, a good man, and the flour we will get. Look, I have money. I didn't give it all away this time."

Mama could only nod.

"Feed the children and tell them bedtime stories, Margaret," Papa instructed as he climbed in his place behind the steering wheel. Mama was tying the dry scarf around her swollen face as they rode off in the Model-T. Papa was home. All would be well.

Papa interrupted our memories of bygone days, saying, "Ja, Mama worried more about the flour than her tooth. She could have died from the infection but God knew I could never live without her."

Moments later, Papa pulled off the main road, his excitement mounting. "Look Margaret, there is the Thompson farm. Good people, quiet, hard working. They have two sons, Trygvie and Seivert — fine boys."

And so it came to pass there in Canada that I stood proudly beside Papa as he stood in his place meticulously dressed in his black suit and high starched collar, his black shoes polished to a high sheen. He told the farmers who were gathered together, "Today we pitch a tent, but one day there will be a church here with its steeple rising to the sky."

I watched the big-boned Norwegian men take their hammers and drive in the tent stakes; then the large green tent was stretched over the prairie grass. Rough hands held rumpled hats while heads bowed in prayer. Papa's voice boomed confidently, "Lord, bless the world through these, your faithful children. Amen."

2

The Farm

ANOTHER DAY HAD COME to a close, and the Thompson farm seemed to settle into the stillness of the night. Sounds from the chicken house blended into the darkness like a gentle lullaby. The cattle and horses shifted restlessly in the barns, tired after a long day of work.

Mrs. Thompson, a quiet woman with a warm smile, patiently washed the supper dishes while I dried them and kept up a running conversation about life with Mama and the children. Mr. Thompson, still dressed in his work boots and overalls, chuckled as he stacked the wood behind the cookstove in preparation for the next day's early breakfast. Finally he stretched, caught his thumbs on his shoulder straps and peered at me over the tip of his glasses. "Margaret, Margaret, such a life in the Tweten house."

I turned away shyly. The cows had been milked, and

I had helped to wash and scald the separator. Freshly churned butter stood in a crock. Loaves of bread lined the pantry shelf. Jars of homemade strawberry jam stood in rows. Mama would be proud of me.

I filled the water bucket at the pump and hung up the dishtowels to dry. Chores were done and the evening meal was over.

The Thompson boys, Trygvie and Seivert, discussed tomorrow's work with their father. Finally Mr. Thompson pulled off his boots and said good night. Mrs. Thompson took off her starched apron and with a weary sigh followed her husband to the loft.

It was still early, but quiet, gentle, hard-working Trygvie stifled a yawn. Soon he, too, said good night. Papa had gone to visit a neighbor and would be home later. It never occurred to Papa to go to bed before midnight — "So many books to read," he said.

That left only Seivert and me. Seivert, the youngest, seventeen years old with merry blue eyes, seemed to be the only one with an adventurous spirit. He had big-boned, Norwegian features, yet his unruly brown hair framed a boyish face. Seivert had boundless energy and seemed to work effortlessly all day.

He lit the gas lamp on the round table and handed me a book — a paperback novel with a hero, heroine and villain. Seivert's deep blue eyes sparkled with mischief as he confided, "This is what I like to do when everyone goes to bed — read!" An old Victrola stood beside the table and he put on the only record he owned — "Beautiful Ohio." When the record player ran down, Seivert cranked it again and went right on reading.

I had grown up under the protective banner of the parsonage and was well-versed in theology, but the novel offered me a new burst of excitement. I was totally absorbed in Mrs. Southwick's classic — my eyes glued to the pages as the characters, particularly Jack the villain, came alive for me. Too late, a step behind us alerted me to Papa's presence. He was reading over my shoulder. He snatched the book from my hand. Papa glared at Seivert, then back at me. "Margaret, God gave you a good head to read good books. This is foolishness." When he took the book, I was right at the best part, where the hero rescues the heroine.

Years later I asked Papa how the story ended. Before he realized the trap I had set for him, he told me.

There were more paperback books to read that summer, but I made sure I had a "good book" handy — just in case Papa came home.

In the morning the Thompson men ate a hearty breakfast after chores were done, then headed to the fields.

Plows and horses were a familiar sight over the vast prairie, but the Thompsons owned a tractor. My eyes were always on Seivert. He was a hero to me because he drove the tractor and allowed me to ride on it. Up and down the long rows he rode, turning the soft earth. As the rich soil sprayed the air, the birds and small animals scurried to the woods.

I was glad when Mrs. Thompson allowed me to take coffee and bread to the men in the field. I would sit under a tree with Seivert where we shared coffee and a piece of bread. Seivert was my first love. We talked about the big world beyond the farm, and I told him about Winnipeg, the center for immigration trains. I wanted him to see the smoke rising from the engine, hear the train wheels rattling over the rails and watch the lonely, tired Norwegian immigrants stepping from the train into their new world. I told him the story about a missionary barrel and high-button shoes — my life's most valuable lesson.

"Missionary barrel?" he asked. "What's that?"

"A round wooden barrel full of hand-me-downs."

"Just for preachers' children to wear?"

"At least for the Tweten children," I answered defensively. "That's where I got the high-button shoes."

Seivert eyed his own work boots solemnly. "What's the difference as long as they are comfortable?"

"High-button shoes were out," I answered indignantly. "Oxfords were *in*."

I ignored his insensitivity and told him I would be a missionary and see the world and write stories. Seivert shared his dream of a big farm of his own.

I didn't tell Seivert that I cried in my pillow when people laughed at my missionary dreams and jokingly teased that I'd probably be an actress. Papa was always shocked! He assured me that it was his place to keep foolish ideas like acting out of my head. And Mama saw to it that I read good books and practiced the piano.

In my own heart and mind, I reasoned that if I couldn't read novels, then I would write my own stories and poems, and no one would know. Besides, since I was going to be a missionary nurse and see the world, there would be much to write about.

But for now, here on the Canadian prairies, Seivert was my hero! He drove a tractor, read novels and gave me coffee from his jug. Life was good.

3

The Tent Meetings

THE TENT STOOD SILHOUETTED against the clouded Canadian sky. Nearby the open country wagons rumbled over rutted roads.

For days, farm homes had bustled with excitement. Women baked extra bread, and treadle machines worked beyond the call of duty to sew new dresses. Houses were immaculate for overnight guests — perhaps even the preacher.

It was tent-meeting time, and all the people were one. They had shared the toil of the land, the care of the animals, the long winters and the blizzards.

Together, the immigrants grieved over lonely graves and rejoiced over new births. For these people, life and death, agony and ecstasy were a part of life, like sun and rain.

31

With a raw, stubborn courage the men fought for the land to yield, and built homes and barns for shelter from life's storms. For the nourishment of spirit and soul, they built schools and churches. Without murmuring, they held their dreams in their hearts, while rough hands toiled long to make the dreams come true.

The Scandinavian women, with their clear blue eyes and corn-silk hair, worked beside their men, bore their children, provided food from gardens, and kept the family home a place of comfort and shelter. With quiet faith in God they nourished their families with hope. With the coming of each spring they also shared hope for a good crop, laying hens, and playful colts and calves on wobbling legs.

The long winter had passed. Spring had come just like Mama said: "When winter comes, the next thing to come is spring — then the summer. So . . . the bluebirds come, the bluebirds of promise and happiness. So it is with the winter of the soul. It, too, will pass, and the next thing to come is spring — hope springs in the heart."

The winter had passed and spring had ushered in the summer of 1928.

The children ran to do the chores so the evening meal could be served earlier than usual. Even the cows cooperated with early milking.

Now a shiny car stood beside the wagons and buggies — Papa's Model-T held a place of honor. Papa, dressed in his black suit and high starched collar, welcomed the Scandinavian settlers to the summer tent meeting.

Young and old filled the tent — sturdy Norwegian men with thick blond hair and work-worn hands, and women in their new dresses and hand-knit shawls. Children, scrubbed and starched, sat beside their parents while babies slept on quilts under old wooden benches.

Cora Salen took her place at the small pump organ. Then Papa, in his place behind the wooden pulpit, announced the opening hymn: "A Mighty Fortress Is Our

God."

While the babies slept the mothers sang of another day when all would be free from their labors.

Some hymns were sung in Norwegian, others in English — sometimes both at the same time. God understood.

The men sang "Work for the Night Is Coming" with unusual gusto, for they knew, only too well, the hours of toil before darkness covered their fields of grain.

Papa called on Deacon Salen to pray. Deacon Salen was an angular, raw-boned man with bushy eyebrows and a thick mustache. I didn't mind his long prayer because I sat with Seivert and the other young people in the back of the tent. Sitting with Seivert, I was glad that Cora was at the organ. The prayer went on endlessly — partly in English, mostly in Norwegian. While he prayed, we wrote notes to one another deciding who would walk with whom after "meeting." In the middle of the prayer, Deacon Salen peeked and caught us passing notes, then thundered for God to save the young people. We bowed our heads and shuddered, expecting God to strike with lightning force.

When the deacon complained to Papa that the young people were doomed, disrespectful and irreverent, Papa answered, "Ja, ja, Deacon Salen, but we must remember that they are here and they will remember; they are hearing the message. They will be the leaders of the community."

Cora continued to pump the organ for the meetings. Papa continued to stand in his place leading the singing. We sang, "Showers of blessing, showers of blessing we need."

One night the showers came!

Thunder and lightning joined with the enthusiastic singing of "When the roll is called up yonder, I'll be there." We sang louder and louder to the background of peals of thunder added to Cora's organ. The horses kicked and whinnied as the "showers of blessing" fell. Rain and wind blew through the tent flaps. Puddles of water formed on the sawdust trail.

Finally, Papa dismissed the meeting. Horses were unhitched from the wagons as mud and rain made the roads impassable. Some people rode horseback while others sloshed to the nearest farmhouse, their babies wrapped in blankets. The tent was collapsing.

The young people pulled off shoes and stockings and proceeded to walk home barefoot, laughing and shouting. I walked with Seivert. Papa's car stood alone by the empty wagons.

No one would forget the night of the rain. Laughter and stories about that night would fill many lonely winter nights during the months to come.

Within a few days the wind and sun dried up the roads and tent meeting time continued. Papa blessed new babies and baptized converts while we sang, "Yes, we'll gather at the river." There were weddings to perform and funerals to hold. Up and down the country road, the faithful Model-T wound its way into farmyards, and Papa brought laughter and stories into lonely homes. He strummed his guitar and sang the old Norwegian songs. He brought hope and courage where sorrow had been, and renewed faith in God where "believing" had grown dim.

After several weeks it was time to think about going home. Harvest time was coming, with the golden grain waving in the sun. Farmers' wives were lining the cellars with jars of fruit, vegetables, pickles and jam, and the barns began to fill.

The school bell would soon sound out across the fields to call children and books together. There would be a better tomorrow for them.

It was time for me to go back to school, too. The tent must come down for another year.

I sat beside Papa in the Model-T Ford, the box of clothes on my lap. Mama would be proud — Papa had had his white starched shirt for Sunday meetings. Goodbyes and a closing prayer were said. "God be with you till we meet again," echoed across the open fields.

I looked back to wave at Seivert standing beside the tractor, his curly hair caught in the breeze. "I'll miss you," he called. "Come back next year for the tent meeting."

Next year I would be thirteen. I promised to come back.

But Papa's thoughts weren't on seeing Seivert again or on my reading another novel. He was excited about returning to Saskatoon. "Ja, ja, Margaret, now it is time to go home to Mama."

I never went back to that Canadian prairie. When we came home to Mama there was a letter for Papa asking him to be the pastor of the Logan Square Norwegian Baptist Church in Chicago, Illinois.

I cried into my pillow. I knew a page was turning in my life's book. Mama dragged her feet. She didn't want to leave her yellow house in Saskatoon or her new red linoleum. Papa challenged her with God's will. Finally, Mama fought a battle to believe — and won. "Ja, trust and obey. That is the only way," she admitted.

Papa was jubilant! He was going home — home to Chicago where he had studied, home to the libraries and throb of a big city. He was like a restless thoroughbred, anxious for the race. No one ever knew how much he had longed for the great universities, music and stimulating conversation with other theologians. Papa was going to his place.

Mama and her children followed in obedience to God, but the winds of the prairies cried through the waving fields.

I hear the coyote cry
Across the waving grain.
My horse picked up the gait
To race against the rain.

The road was rough and wet;

Wind blew rain like tears.
My heart would never forget
The prairie's passing years.

I knew a childish love,
A friend, the prairie sound!
Wind blowing clouds above;
A country lane — hallowed ground.

Now — a dusty window pane
Washed with childish tears;
The lonely whistle of a train
Rolling past my prairie years.

September 1928

4

Papa's Church, Chicago

July 1984.

I WAS GOING BACK to Papa's church! My husband, Harold, eased the car out of the driveway while our two grandsons Shawn and Eric curled up in sleeping bags in the back of our station wagon. It was 2 A.M., a quiet time to drive. But for me, it was a time to go a long way back — to the year 1928 to the train ride from Saskatoon, Saskatchewan, to Chicago, Illinois.

Along the railroad tracks friendly grownups smiled and children waved as the five Tweten children pressed their faces against the soot-covered windows. Papa was rejoicing. Mama was thoughtful — and afraid. She was afraid of the gangsters, the dirt, the noise — and she was sad to leave the first house of her own, her gardens, and her prized possession, the red linoleum. But she had prayed. God had spoken to her heart and she was a child of God who walked in obedience.

Fear thou not; for I am with thee:
be not dismayed; for I am thy God:
I will strengthen thee; yea,
I will help thee,
Yea, I will uphold thee with the
right hand of my righteousness (Isaiah 41:10).

When God spoke to Mama out of His Word, Mama believed and obeyed.

I was sad as the cold, smoky train rattled over the rails, carrying me away from the familiar to a new adventure. When the train pulled in at the Union Station in Chicago, I saw a city of a million lights. We clung to Mama in terror, for this was the city of gangsters. We didn't know what gangsters were, but the way people talked, we knew they had to be bad.

The Chicago wind blew dust and debris everywhere, and the noise was deafening. Papa was like a bird out of a cage. He loved the sound of the city. "Isn't this wonderful?" he shouted above the noise and din. We agreed. No one argued with Papa.

The two deacons who met us drove shiny cars with glass windows. The Knudsons took Mama, Papa, Doris and baby Joyce Solveig with them. The Pete Rossings took Grace, Gordon and me. Mama whispered confidential orders to me about "helping." "Be sure no one sees the children's dirty underwear from our sooty train ride," she warned. The ministry, I well understood, must never be disgraced — especially by soiled underwear. I assured Mama I would "help."

The ride was terrifying. People and cars were everywhere; even young children were out at night. Didn't Chicago have a 9 o'clock curfew? Where were all the people going? I had only ridden country roads with Papa in his Model-T, and this was a ride I would never forget. I held Grace and Gordon close to me.

When we arrived at the Rossing house, the fears melted in the warmth of their loving reception. I had never seen anything so beautiful. A veranda encircled the house and the spacious rooms were elegant in beauty and order. The most marvelous thing was the gleaming white kitchen. But where was the cookstove?

Somehow, I missed the four-room yellow house with the cookstove and rocking chair. Life seemed so safe with Mama and Papa in the small house where we were all close together.

The sounds of the elevated trains and street cars came crashing in. Besides, I had to help. Like Mama always said, "Just do what you have to do." I had to take care of the children.

My thoughts were interrupted by Harold's comments about the road detours and his suggestion, "Look for a place to eat breakfast." Our grandsons, blond and blue-eyed with Southern accents, emerged from their sleeping bags and dressed in a hurry. A Shoney's Breakfast Buffet sign, blazing in the sky, gave the needed motivation.

As we ate, my husband said, "I think Shawn is bottomless, Margaret. That's his third plate!" We laughed together as we relished the good coffee and beautiful buffet. Too soon it was time to hit the road.

"How long until we get to Uncle Steve's?" the boys asked.

"Not too long."

The boys read road maps and brushed up on geography as we drove to Nashville, Tennessee, where we would visit Uncle Steve and Aunt Beverly and the two young cousins, Benjamin and Paul.

The hour finally came when we were all entangled

in hugs and laughter. Uncle Steve shouted, "I can't believe you guys — going to Chicago to visit your great-grandfather's church! You'll never forget this trip!"

I knew Steve was right; none of us would ever forget. Too soon we were on the road again. The hours and miles sped by until it was evening, time to find a motel. The swimming pool meant more than Chicago at that time.

While Shawn and Eric swam, I wrote in my journal: "I am retracing my steps, going into the past — back to my father's places of service. I'm beginning in Chicago where I'll be speaking from Papa's same pulpit. Papa would like that. Next year I hope to go to Wisconsin to visit his first church, then to Canada, and finally the greatest thrill of all — Norway. That is my dream — Norway! But I wonder how I can ever go there? Somehow, I know I will. I must go back to my roots and with going back, gain a greater understanding of my restless, impatient, independent father." I closed my journal. My thoughts went faster than my pen.

It was late when Harold and the boys fell asleep. My thoughts drifted back to another day. . .

Papa had found a second-floor flat, not too far from the Logan Square Baptist Church. We had to take our shoes off and walk quietly, so as not to disturb the tenants on the first floor. The flat had steam heat and hot water — a luxury we had never dreamed of.

I had my own clean water for the Saturday night bath, and didn't have to bathe in a round tub in the kitchen.

Mama had managed to get the treadle sewing machine on the moving van when Papa wasn't looking. She quickly put it in a corner of the flat and covered it with a fancy embroidered cloth.

Papa had insisted that electric sewing machines were used in Chicago and had promised to buy Mama one. But she knew the money would go for books and she wouldn't see an electric machine.

"Just some things Papa doesn't understand," Mama defended as she told us to be quiet about the treadle machine. "Better to have a treadle machine, than no machine." Mama was always right.

Papa had his books and desk. He had his libraries to study in, his pulpit to preach from, a congregation who loved him — and Mama. Papa was in his place.

The lonely soon found their way to the second-floor flat. We learned to play in alleys and walk to the library to study.

Papa lived in his world. It was up to God and Mama to take care of the children in a real world.

Then we had to move! The Great Depression brought changes to everyone. Mama found a cold-water flat where we heated the house with a stove in the parlor and a garbage burner in the kitchen. The water had to be heated by gas — and that was expensive. Mama kept big kettles of water on the stoves.

Papa was oblivious to the changes. He still had his desk, his books and his warm libraries to study in. Now we slept three in a bed. Doris slept in the middle to keep warm; Grace slept by the wall. I was the oldest and it was up to me to keep from falling out when we turned together. The room was just large enough for the one bed and one small dresser. Grace, Doris and I had one drawer each.

The welcome sound came each morning at 5 A.M. when Papa shook the stove and sang, "Standing on the Promises." Doris, Grace and I snuggled under our home-made quilts. We had another hour to sleep while Papa got the house warm.

Finally I heard Papa call, "Come, Margaret — time to get up."

I dressed quickly. Clothes were always laid out the night before. When I went into the warm kitchen, Papa was in the rocking chair reading his Bible. I went quickly to the table where Papa had hot cocoa and six slices of oven toast ready. I ate in silence while Papa read.

With a "Takk for maten,"(Thanks for the food), I buttoned up my coat.

Looking over his rimless glasses Papa said, "Velkecommen," (You're welcome) and, "button up your collar. It's cold." He went back to reading and I set out on the three-mile walk to Carl Schurz High School.

My friend who walked to school with me made her own breakfast. No one was up to say, "Button up your coat — it's cold." I felt safe and loved. It was 6:45 A.M., still dark and cold outside. We walked because the street car ride was too expensive — a whole nickel — and we carried our lunches in bags. We were happy to be friends. Life was good.

Before I knew it, Harold was rousing us so we could get on the road. "Chicago, here we come!" he announced.

The easy living of summertime at Wrightsville Beach, North Carolina, was a far cry from the sounds of Chicago with its moving masses of people, its towering skyscrapers, and the sight of Lake Michigan rolling over the rocks.

Shawn and Eric moved through museums, parks, industrial science buildings, and traffic jams with screeching cars; they rode to the top of the Sears tower, and they were fascinated by the elevated trains and the police whistles. However, the throbbing sound of the big city came back to me with memories of another day. The sound seemed the same, yet the milk wagons were gone, and I didn't hear the cries of the vendors selling rags and iron. The smell of fresh fish in the alley was missing.

While I was being interviewed by Jim Warren on "Prime Time America," my grandsons were intrigued by the sophisticated equipment in the studio. Later we toured the great Moody Bible Institute where Harold and I had attended evening classes.

I remembered the first programs from Moody's radio

station WMBI — hymns and preaching. In my childhood Papa always allowed all of us to listen to the hymns and preaching, as long as we did our studies and music.

One day when Papa came home, I was doing my homework on the parlor floor. I had switched from WMBI to WLS, the country music station.

Mama and Papa were drinking coffee when Papa asked the usual questions.

"Are the children good, Mama?"

"Ja, the children are good," she said softly.

"Do they practice the piano?"

"Ja, they practice, Papa."

"Are they on the honor roll?"

"Of course!" (God help us if we didn't make it.)

"Mama, are you sure the children listen to good music?"

"Ja, Papa. We only listen to Moody."

The sounds from WLS were coming through. Papa sat up, "Mama, I tell you one thing. I think Moody is getting 'vorldly.' " I switched the dial immediately.

The past and present blended as Harold began to ease through the Chicago traffic. An unexpected hail-storm blocked us on an overpass for more than an hour and turned into a great adventure for our two Carolina boys. But the warm welcome into the home of childhood friends, the "Halbom kids," made the traffic jam a faded memory. It didn't seem possible that the adorable, curly-headed girls of yesterday now had children and grandchildren of their own. We laughed together and the years melted like soft snow.

On Sunday morning, I stood in Papa's place.

To the left was the choir loft where we used to sing "Master, the Tempest Is Raging." For a moment, I could almost hear the bass voices again, singing, " 'The winds and the waves shall obey My will. . .' " Back then I had joined Leona, Mrs. Moore, Helen and others in the echo, "Peace, be still!" Hagen's tenor had sounded clear as a bell and Harold Nilsen's bass never faltered. Today many of those voices are stilled, but the song goes on.

I focused on the audience in front of me — so diverse, but all American! Black, brown and white faces, young and old. The blond heads I knew in my youth were now white — and our grandchildren sat beside us. The bulletin board "read" Spanish, instead of Norwegian. The pastor was the Reverend Steve Hasper — not E. N. Tweten. That was another day, another time.

The red brick church on the square stood sandwiched between other brick buildings — but it stood, clean and well preserved. The same gospel message of God's love for all the world still sounded forth from the pulpit. The string band was gone, but the place was there. Once again I heard Papa announce, "Now we will hear from the string band."

Tall Mr. Lundaman stood proudly, tuning his violin as the others came from the back of the church to take their places at the table. It never occurred to anyone to be seated before the service. This was their moment in the sun. All week many worked as housekeepers in the affluent suburbs, but tonight, the Sunday night service, was their moment of glory.

On Tuesday they would travel two hours on elevated trains, street cars or buses to attend the string band practice. Mama played a guitar and someone wrote the chords for her. Harold Nilsen played the mandolin and Han Strom played the zither. There were more guitars and a flute, and Papa saw to it that I played something — a ten-stringed Harmony Tipples (like a ukulele).

We would tune up slowly. No one was in a hurry. Then, with a flourish, Mr. Lundaman would strike up the bow and the music began. "He the Pearly Gates Will Open" was the favorite. Then more songs. Tuesday night string band practice always ended with prayer and coffee — a night of music and laughter.

When it was time to go home, Papa would ride the elevated train with the girls who had come alone to ensure their safety. He was the shepherd and this was his family. It was Papa's place.

When Sunday night came and Papa announced the string band, the cares of the long week were forgotten. The string band was playing, and the congregation singing, "I will meet you in the morning, Just inside the Eastern Gate. Then be ready, faithful pilgrim, Lest with you it be too late."

As I stood behind Papa's pulpit, I found myself saying, "Somehow, I think God parted the curtains of heaven today just to let our loved ones join us as we meet together. I can hear the music of the choirs of long ago, and hear the strumming of guitars. I think the string band of heaven is playing our song, 'When we all get to heaven, What a day of rejoicing that will be!' "

I smiled at "my congregation" and said, "It's a different time, a new people, varied races, but we are all in our place. Jesus Christ alone is the same, yesterday, today, and forever."

There was joy and peace in my heart that Sunday morning, for among the cloud of witnesses from the grandstand of heaven I seemed to see Papa — in his place.

5

Anna

THE 1985 WRITER'S CONFERENCE at Gordon College in Wenhem, Massachusetts, had come to a close, and I was enjoying a relaxed evening with my two eldest grandchildren, Heather, 15, and Chad, 12. Their favorite dinner of southern fried chicken, mashed potatoes, hot biscuits and cherry pie was ready to serve. I was stirring the milk gravy when the telephone rang.

Janice, our daughter, answered. She turned to me and said, "Mom, it's for you. It's Jud."

Dr. Judson Carlberg, Janice's husband and dean of the faculty at Gordon College, was hosting a consortium of college educators from across the country and tonight was their kick-off banquet. A prominent speaker from the West Coast had been scheduled to speak on the theme: "The Integration of Faith and Social Action."

Jud's voice came over the phone, "Mom, the guest speaker missed his plane. Could you be ready in thirty minutes?"

Jan answered for me, "Of course she can be ready."

And so it came to pass that my favorite son-in-law introduced me to a bewildered audience of educators as the "Speaker of the House."

I would probably never address a more profound looking gathering; nevertheless, I began, "Tonight you can become children again for I am just a storyteller." Pens and notebooks disappeared.

"Your theme intrigues me, and the idea of revolutionary ideas sounds exciting. I grew up with revolutionary ideas. My father was a stubborn Norwegian and he seldom did anything the orthodox way.

"Now Mama would like the title, 'The Integration of Faith and Social Action,' only she would say it like this:

'Ja, ja, faith and vorks all go together.

You do vot you have to do.

It is simple — yust not easy.

You trust and obey God,

Love and forgive, do vot is in your hand to do.

It is simple — it is yust not so easy.'

"As for Papa, he did it his way. He probably invented brown bagging." I saw my dignified audience relaxing. I was at ease myself. After all it was a privilege to tell the stories of Mama and Papa — even the stories of the Great Depression.

During the Great Depression some of Papa's church parishioners were patients at the Cook County Hospital in Chicago. They were terrified, not only because of their illness, but also to be considered charity. Depression years brought changes to these proud Norwegians.

"Oh, ja, it won't be so bad," Papa cheerfully assured them. "I come with Mama's soup."

The story was so familiar to me. He took a jar of Mama's homemade soup, wrapped it in a turkish towel and placed it in a brown bag. So began the daily trek of Papa's "brown bagging."

An hour's ride on two street cars brought Papa to the County Hospital. There he read God's promises from the Bible, offered prayer for health and courage, then calmly spoon-fed Mama's soup to the frightened patients. Years later these same people told how they waited for Papa's brown bag and Bible.

Integration of faith and social action? "Ja, ja," Mama would say, "Faith and vorks. It goes together."

One day during the depression, after a hospital visit, Papa passed by the dejected wrecks of humanity huddled in the outpatient clinic. Many had been brought there by the police. Suddenly Papa heard someone call out hysterically in Norwegian.

Papa stopped at the desk, "May I help?" he asked. "I am a Norwegian minister."

"Oh, can you ever help!" the nurse said in a disgruntled tone. "We have a wild woman the police brought in and no one can understand her." She nodded toward a large, blonde woman in the corner. "Perhaps you can reason with her. We are getting ready to transfer her to a mental hospital."

"Let me see what I can do first."

When Papa spoke to the frightened woman in her own language, she calmed down enough to tell her story: "I went from door to door asking for vork. I vork," she said. "But when one resident discovered her jewels were missing, she called the police and told them, 'A crazy-looking woman came here looking for work. She has to be the thief!' "

Unable to explain in English, the frightened woman became hysterical as the police dragged her to the station for questioning. She finally became unmanageable. She was taken from the jail to the Cook County Clinic where plans were made to transfer her to the mental hospital.

Papa listened patiently as he gathered the bits and pieces of the story. When he heard all of it, he strode over to the director of the clinic, his blue eyes blazing, "I vill tell you vun t'ing. This voman is not crazy. She is Norwegian!"

"Will you sign for her release?" the director asked.

Papa grabbed the pen. "Of course, I vill sign!"

In the meantime at home, Mama had supper ready. "Margaret, look out the window and see if Papa is coming." The worry lines on her face deepened.

I looked. "He's coming, Mama, but you should see what he has with him!"

Mama shook her head. "Put another plate on the table, Grace. Papa has company."

Moments later, Papa stood before us, tall and dignified in his black suit, black hat and high starched collar. Clinging to his arm was a large woman, her coat bulging at the seams, her slip sagging. I stared at her. High above her forehead, on top of her blond hair perched a hat with a feather sticking up, and on her bare, squatty legs, cotton stockings were rolled down around her ankles.

She clung tenaciously to Papa's arm. "This wonderful man," she exclaimed in Norwegian, "This wonderful man! They said I was crazy but he told them I was Norwegian. How did you ever find such a wonderful man?"

Mama hid a smile as if to say, "Oh, we'll talk about that wonderful man later." (We had all thought it was the other way around.)

We stared open-mouthed at the apparition before us. With steely blue eyes, Papa glared at us, "Say hello to Anna, children!"

Quickly recovering, we all shook hands with a formal, "Velkomen, Anna."

We sat down at the table and we asked a Norwegian

blessing in unison. After the meal Mama asked Papa quietly, "Well, Papa, what do we do now?"

Papa frowned; then his bushy eyebrows arched. "Anna will stay with us until I can find another way. I'll think about it tomorrow. We take one day at the time."

So Anna slept on the parlor sofa. The next day Papa took two street cars to see Mrs. Farmen who had clothes large enough for Anna. Finding a home for Anna took longer. Finally Papa came home with the announcement that he had found a home for her.

Anna became the dishwasher in a Norwegian mission house for immigrant girls. She had her own room, and, best of all, a family. She spent her life there, productive and happy.

When Sunday mornings came, she sat in the front of the church, never taking her eyes off that "wonderful man."

The parlor sofa was empty once more, but not for long. Papa would come again and again with someone for the sofa. My eyes swept over my audience of profound and learned educators. With my heart I saw caring people who longed to reach out to a crying world of Annas. "But we must do it God's way," I concluded.

"When our boats are loosed from our moorings in Christ Jesus, we become victims to the tide of man's philosophy. But if we follow Mama's faith, Mama's philosophy, we can say,

'Ja, ja, faith and vorks go together.

Trust and obey God.

Love and forgive everyone.

Do vot you have to do.

Do vot is in your hand —

Yust *do it*!

It is so simple — it is yust not easy.'

"God bless you all."

The following day I was on my way home to North

Carolina. Within a few weeks the family would gather for a happy reunion at beautiful Wrightsville Beach.

The weeks flew by and once again that summer of 1985, we enjoyed our shrimp and cornbread, garden vegetables and homemade ice cream. When we watched the sun-tanned grandchildren race down the sandy beach and jump into the sunlit waves, we were remembering our own children when they were young. It was as though we were seeing Jan, Dan and Ralph race ahead of us to hit the beach first.

Wasn't it only yesterday?

Staring at the waters at Wrightsville Beach, past and present merged again. Somewhere on the backroads of my mind, I heard Papa's church singing: "Wonderful the matchless Grace of Jesus, deeper than the mighty rolling sea . . ."

6

Woodville, 1985

THE PLANE SOARED over the mountains and valleys of North Carolina. Shawn, our thirteen-year-old grandson, sat with his face glued to the window. The clouds rolled like sunlit cotton into the blue expanse around us.

Within a few days we would be in Papa's first church in Woodville, Wisconsin. I would be a part of the celebration of the church's 100th anniversary.

At the moment it was enough to watch my grandson enjoy his first plane trip. Deep within me, I had a dream of taking the grandchildren, one by one, to journey with me into the past.

When we arrived in Minneapolis, we were enveloped within the love and warmth of Bill Swanson, his lovely wife Wilma and their three children. Bill had been a part of our ministry — Harold's and mine.

Thirty seven years ago a lonely, bewildered teenager sat in my kitchen watching me bake bread and roll out pie crusts. Bill complained that cookie dough was just as good before the baking — so why wait? His loneliness was soon replaced by God's unfailing love through Jesus Christ, and Harold encouraged Bill to pursue his education. Now, we were guests in his lovely home. God's big circle has room for an ever-expanding family.

Within a few days we were on the road to Woodville, Wisconsin, a quaint town of Norwegian descendants, about an hour's drive from Minneapolis. The road dipped and curved around the rolling fields of grain, past old farmhouses nestled in groves of white birch and towering blue spruce.

Mooing cows with full udders headed slowly down a country lane to the barn. Clucking chickens and playful kittens followed the farmer and his milk pail. Streaks of red and gold sent signals across the sky to announce the closing of another day.

I watched the town come into view and soon spotted the white church steeple reaching into the evening sky. Across the street stood the old parsonage framed with flower boxes — geraniums mixed with blue delphiniums and yellow marigolds. Mildred and Walter Obbink rocked contently on the squeaking porch swing.

"Ja," the elderly couple said, "this is where you were born, Margaret. Not too much changed." *Except there's a bathroom in the front hall,* I thought, *and the cookstove is gone.* In its place stood an electric stove — with a coffee pot on it. We sat down for coffee.

"So this is where Papa brought Mama, and where I was born!" I repeated, and sipped my coffee. Steam from my cup rose with my memories. I wondered what dreams Mama had at twenty-one — or were fears hidden in her heart? What dreams did Papa have when he brought his bride to this Scandinavian town?

Seventy years had passed since then. I found myself

looking at the place where the stove used to stand and I remembered how Mama burned the dress. It had been a new spring dress, not one of somber brown or black, but a soft delicate pink with lace and a wide sash. Papa saw the dress as foolishness and pride. In anger he destroyed the dress and Mama's dream. Her wounded spirit finally calmed when she learned that God's forgiveness included destroying the evidence. I could almost hear her say, "I'm burning the evidence. Love and forgive, love and forgive."

Within my heart I said, "Thank you, Mama."

At last I was able to focus on Mildred Obbink's electric stove. Mama's old wood stove faded away — but not my memories.

Within a few hours I found myself behind Papa's pulpit, looking into the faces of a packed church. Returning missionaries and ministers told of their decisions made in this church to live for God. I heard stories of young people who had gone out into a more challenging world but who remembered their foundational roots in God's love and family traditions.

Elderly people remembered me, the first baby born to the young Tweten preacher and his lovely wife. "I used to rock you," one lady said.

Another added, "Your Papa would hitch up the horse and buggy and your Mama tied you around her waist. Then they would visit between Baldwin and Woodville."

"Your Mama started the young people's work and everyone loved her readings and stories," someone else told me.

"Ja, I vas young," another one said, "but I remember you."

From Papa's pulpit I shared the stories about my parents and told about "Mama's children." The audience laughed and cried while we remembered together.

The psalmist says in Psalm 78 that "the fathers should show the generations to come the praises of the Lord."

Tonight we were remembering that the God of our fathers was our God. The Rock of Ages was our Rock in the time of storm. I wanted my grandchildren to know that.

Looking into the beautiful faces before me, I told the people at Papa's church, "Papa's seven children love the same God because Papa taught that Jesus Christ is the Way, the Truth and the Life. And because Mama took us by the hand and walked with us in paths of righteousness."

All too soon, the sign, "Velkommen to Woodville" faded into the distance. It was time to return to our home in North Carolina where the ocean rolls across the sun-kissed shore.

The timeless ocean reminds me of the unlimited grace of God. The quaint Woodville village, with flower boxes on the parsonage, reminded me of the faithfulness of God. The open Bible on Papa's pulpit was another reminder that throughout all life's changes, God's Word is forever settled in heaven.

In my journal I wrote, "Jesus Christ — the same yesterday, and today and forever" (Hebrews 13:8). You can go home again — even back to painful memories, where God's redemptive love heals and restores the past. I did!

7

The Storm

BEFORE MAMA'S HOMEGOING on January 14, 1977, she shared the story of "The Dress" in her wonderful way. There was only love and understanding in her portrayal of Papa. She must have thought it was important for future generations or she would have kept the story sealed within her heart.

To me, it reveals again the marvelous grace of God, the love of our heavenly Father as well as man's frailty in life's storms.

One writer said, "We beat our boats against a current to go back." Yet I find myself choosing to flow with the current toward the future.

So, reluctantly, I turn my boat into the current to go back and take you with me to a place and time as it *might* have been. Somehow in the gathering of bits and pieces I see it as though it really happened this way.

Back to Woodville, seventy years ago. Back to the year 1917 when Papa, a young preacher in his first church, raced over the country roads on his horse. He was always in a hurry to fulfill his tasks. That day, he was as restless as the wind. Cows and chickens, horses and pigs, crops and weather were the topics of each day.

He was remembering his boyhood days in Norway: cows and chickens, horses and pigs, crops and weather — the same. In Norway, after early morning chores, he had run the four miles to school, over the rocky mountain roads to the place of books and learning. Always he dreamed of a time he would have books and more books to study, and he would learn all he could.

Then that time had come! At seventeen years of age, he enrolled in the Baptist Theological Seminary affiliated with Chicago University.

Now, in Woodville, everything within him cried out for the throbbing city of Chicago. As he rode, he remembered sleeping in the furnace room and being the automatic stoker for the huge furnaces. Mr. Anderson, the cook, had brought waffles and coffee to keep him awake.

Papa had his books, the vast resources of a great library. There were other scholars with whom to enjoy stimulating discussions and share ideas. There were museums, art galleries, parks, concerts and people of all races with differing views.

And there was the great Moody Bible Institute with its scholarly Bible teachers, and its access to his favorite reading — Spurgeon's volumes.

Papa's horse trotted along the country road in Woodville, keeping step with thoughts that went stepping into the past. He felt a twinge of regret at the memory of selling Mama's piano for books. He knew it was Mama's own upright piano, bought with her own money, before their marriage — money earned as a maid. It did not seem important that she had not run her fingers over the keyboard once more before he sold it. *But surely any sensible woman could see the value of books,* he argued with himself. *The piano could wait.* Then creeping into his memory was the money for the wedding picture. He used that for books, too. A picture could wait. (It would wait until their fiftieth wedding anniversary.)

The horse raced faster and the restless rider became more frustrated. "I must have books!" he shouted to the wind. "I can't live without books! Surely there must be a way to save money — and I need a new lamp for reading late at night."

When Papa rode along the road, he stopped at farms, listened to the farmers' daily woes about crops and cows, read Scripture, prayed for the families, comforted the lonely and sick, and brought news from town to town. There was always time for a cup of coffee and for some stories to bring laughter and joy to the homes of this strong, productive community. He loved all those people and was a part of them, but that day he felt like a dry well. His usual ruddy complexion was pasty, his quick smile restrained.

He wondered if any of them really understood the time and effort he put into his sermons, the planned outlines, the research into Greek and Hebrew. Still, in church, the farmers nodded and the women and children listened politely. Then there was Mama's face in the audience. Her glowing expression never wavered, eyes brimming with pride and her hands folded in prayer. To her, each sermon was his best.

But he was dry. He needed fresh springs of water — books! That was what he needed! His restless spirit mingled with a complaining spirit. Self pity edged in with cruel cunning. Now he was angry — angry to be without a challenge, cut off from stimulating resources. And now there was a new baby on the way and that meant even less money.

Wasn't this how it was when he was a child in

Norway? Sickness and death, hard work, loneliness and fear. But he'd had his school books — his best friend. And his guitar. Even that was gone, though, given to his sister when he left Norway for America.

Papa felt empty! This wasn't how he dreamed it would be. He dreamed of greater opportunities, universities — perhaps teaching. He dreamed of challenging audiences, travel — and more books!

The horse trotted at an even pace but now Papa was angry — angry at circumstances. Angry at God.

"After all, I have given my life to serve You, God, and now I am back where I used to be — crops and cows." Sadness engulfed him. He would go home — home to Mama for a cup of coffee. Perhaps Mama had saved some money and he could get books. That was it. Perhaps Mama would have the answer, the money. He turned his horse around, but the anger mounted within him.

At home Mama held up the dress. It was finished. One-year-old Margaret squealed with delight as Mama twirled in her billowing skirt of soft pink voile with tiny violets. The lace collar and cuffs, and the wide sash made the new dress a creation of beauty.

Mama loosened her soft brown hair and danced in joyous abandonment. She had managed to save enough money for the dress material as well as a new lamp for Papa.

The long winter was over. The breeze blew softly through Mama's starched curtains. She was tired of black and brown dresses, befitting the ministry, tired of having her hair up in a bun. After all, she was only twenty-three. And it was spring.

She couldn't wait to show off for her handsome, unpredictable husband. The baby within her stirred. She sang joyously.

Before Mama realized how time had flown, she heard the galloping hoofs of Papa's horse. The door opened. Her heart leaped. Papa was home — and she twirled around in the billowing softness of voile and violets.

Suddenly, without warning, the storm broke! Blinded by fury, Papa saw only that the last hope for books was gone. "Foolishness, foolishness," he cried, "when I need books!" The rage within him exploded and the dress was left in shreds. Then he jumped on his horse and galloped away in unbridled anger.

The house of springtime became silent with only the mourning of a winter wind.

Like a wounded bird, Mama moaned in agony of soul and body. Then she gathered the tattered dress and placed the remnants safely in a chest. This she would never forget!

Moaning in pain, she put on the black dress and rolled her hair back up in a bun. When night came she put Papa's supper in the warming oven, gathered up the baby and climbed up to the loft. With her child in her arms, she curled up on a pallet and made her plans to leave Papa — for a season. She would return to the security of her mother, Bertilda, in Brooklyn. She knew she would never leave Papa permanently but she needed time to let her wounded spirit heal.

Later that night, Papa came home. For him, the storm had passed and he couldn't understand the foolishness of Mama in the loft. At his command, Mama quietly placed the sleeping child in the crib and took her place beside Papa.

The following days she put one foot ahead of the other, doing routine tasks as a God-given blessing for survival. There were floors to scrub, clothes to wash, endless meals to cook, not only for the family, but for the visiting minister, Pastor Hanson.

Papa was jubilant! Pastor Hanson, the guest speaker for the church conference, was a welcome companion in conversation and books.

The routine order of living went on — Mama's sparkling windows covered with starched curtains, the embroidered tablecloth with dainty coffee cups, a happy child playing with a string of empty spools of thread, the smell of freshly baked bread — and Mama in a crisp apron. The message came across that all was well.

No one suspected the dark night of her soul as she waited for the moment to show Pastor Hanson the dress. Then she could go to Brooklyn! Mama would wait.

Papa, oblivious to Mama's agony, lived in his world with a new zest for life.

The right moment never came! Pastor Hanson's sermon on love and forgiveness came crashing in on Mama's soul. "Love and forgive," cried out to be heard. "Destroy the evidence," rang as a bell from the church steeple.

Across the pages of time came the living Word from the heart of God to Mama's heart. "When you stand praying, forgive."

"No, No! I can't forgive! I can't forgive!" Mama protested.

The words seemed to thunder in Mama's ears: "Forgive us our trespasses as we forgive those who trespass against us."

Louder and clearer came the words that burned into her soul: "When you stand praying, forgive."

Back into the hidden recesses of her mind came the distant memories of her mother and grandmother making difficult choices. They chose to leave the scene of heartbreak and discover a new life. Was that the choice for her also? Should she leave Papa?

"Oh, God, where do I go, except to Thee. Out of my depths I cry to Thee. Lead me in Your way — the path of trust and obedience; the way of love and forgiveness — unconditional love and forgiveness. Only within me can God bring a new beginning. There is no place to flee — only to the Rock of Ages."

The service was concluded and Mama moved quickly from the church to the horse and buggy, the child tied to her waist. With a snap of the reins, she sped homeward.

Placing the baby in the crib, she reached into the

chest for the tattered dress. Holding it to her tear-stained face she offered the dress to God, a sacrifice of the heart. "For You, dear Lord," she whispered. She opened the lid of the stove and held the dress above the flame. "When you forgive, you destroy the evidence," sounded within her.

She heard a familiar step behind her. She turned. There stood Papa, a bewildered expression on his face. "What are you doing?" he asked.

"I am burning the evidence!" Mama dropped the tattered dress into the flame. *Mama had made a choice — to obey God!*

Stunned by the sudden realization of what he had done, Papa murmured, "Forgive me, Mama."

Pastor Hanson left. No one ever knew this story until Mama told it herself before she went home to stand in the dress God made for her, His robe of righteousness.

I was the baby, Margaret Louise, and the new life within Mama became my sister, Bernice. The choice Mama made that day was the "molten moment" of her life — a covenant with God, the God of promise who never fails.

8

The Ruth Fest

"HAROLD, WOULD YOU PLEASE HELP with the lighting of candles at the Christmas Eve service?" Sarah Durham asked my husband.

"Oh no, I'm sorry," he answered. "We can't break tradition. Christmas Eve at home is an old Norwegian custom." Rolling his eyes toward the heavens, he smiled, "Besides what would Mama and Papa think?"

"Oh, come on Dad, lets' change it — just a little," Janice pleaded.

When our daughter looked at her father with her big brown eyes, he'd go to any length to please her. That is how we found ourselves at the Myrtle Grove Presbyterian Church on Christmas Eve, 1985. Harold was lighting the candles and Sarah Durham was smiling.

Our family sat in a row — Ralph and Chris with

their children Shawn, Eric, Sarah and Kathryn; Janice and Jud with Heather and Chad from Massachusetts. We missed Dan and Virginia who lived in California.

We had been together for a beautiful Christmas Eve dinner in Ralph and Chris's home. After the service, we planned to return there for the opening of gifts and the traditional coffee and Jule kakke.

Christmas Day everyone would come to grandma and grandpa's house. Now we were adding the Candlelight Service to our Christmas traditions.

The church was packed, with chairs in the aisles and the balcony overflowing. The choir and orchestra filled the air with Christmas music and everyone joined in singing the traditional carols.

A message from our beloved pastor, Horace Hilton, brought the service to the lighting of the candles. One by one we held a candle and felt the hush of "O Holy Night."

The candles took me back to another day when the Christmas tree had borne lighted candles. I was remembering how Papa brought home the lonely immigrants from the railroad station to eat lute fisk and rice pudding. I could almost hear their footsteps in the snow.

As my grandchildren sang "Silent Night, Holy Night," their faces blurred and it seemed that I could hear the immigrants singing, "Glade Jule — Helege Jule."

Once again I was rowing my boat of memory against the current, back to the 1930 Ruth Fest. The place was Chicago — at Papa's church in Logan Square. Could it really have been that long ago when I can still see it so clearly?

The Christmas Sunday school program, the event of the year, featured not only talent but also Scandinavian endurance. Mothers spent long nights in close communion with the Singer treadle machine, while children spent hours rehearsing "pieces."

This generation of American-born Norwegians was

expected to perform before a church filled with immigrants and American friends. Mischievous boys in hand-made suits called a holiday truce with the girls in their ruffles and starched petticoats and with bright hairbows bobbing on their shiny blond heads.

Against the background of scented pine, Mama gave her annual Christmas reading, "Annie and Willie's Prayer." In conclusion, each child was given the treasured bag of candy and fruit — and a heart full of memories that would linger throughout the new year.

Every group in Papa's church had a special program — even Mrs. Wiberg's Vorld Vild Girls (World Wide Girls). December began with fests and ended with the New Year's Day annual church fest. Only Christmas Eve belonged to just the family.

No church service compared with the "Root Fest" (Ruth Fest). The Norwegian "Root" girls of the "Root" Society planned all year for this, their night. Many of these single girls worked as housekeepers in the affluent suburban homes and traveled long hours on buses and elevated trains to attend Papa's church.

They banded together and bought a three-flat building in Logan Square. It was their home. The Ruth girls shared their joys and sorrows, reached out to welcome newcomers, and entertained visiting missionaries and ministers.

No one ever told them about the plight of the single girl so they gave themselves to serve others with joyous abandonment. At Sunday school picnics it was the "Root" girls who had an extra nickel for ice cream. When they received clothing from their employers, they graciously gave to those in need — usually Mama's children.

Their guitar music and laughter lingers in my memories of Chicago and Papa's church. Their fest was held in the auditorium of the church. The Christmas tree touched the ceiling. Boughs of pine lined the platform and window sills. The choir sang; the string band played. Hagin Lorentzen sang "The Holy City" and Leona Gjertsen sang

"Have You Any Room For Jesus?" Mama gave a reading, "The Guest."

At the conclusion of the program, everyone was invited to the church basement for refreshments. (Today it is called the fellowship hall.) The basement was decorated with evergreen that had been picked from the forest preserves. In the center stood a large decorated tree. Mr. Lundaman, leader of the string band, tuned up his violin, and the pianists, Eleanor, Hazel and Harriet took turns.

Now the march around the tree began. All year, boys had been eyeing girls in preparation for the annual march. Children of all ages paired up first. Then adults invited American guests to join the newcomers in the march around the tree. Norwegian and American carols echoed into the night as partners changed, and the march reversed. Bowing, clapping, spinning and turning, the church family welcomed the Christmas season in Norwegian style.

The table was prepared for the happy guests. Danish layer cakes and Swedish limpa bread invaded the Norwegian territory of Jule kakke, butter cookies, hard boiled eggs with anchovies, and goat cheese.

The younger generation assisted the elderly for respect was a way of life. The huge coffee pot in the kitchen held the clear amber glow of beaten eggs mixed with coffee grounds and boiled just right. Thick cream and sugar lumps waited to play their part in the celebration.

After the celebration, the "Root" girls, ages nineteen to ninety, had their moment of glory. Tall Berta Herness marched with plump, rosy-cheeked Annie Emerson. The two of them owned a delicatessen. One night, when a robber threatened them, Berta calmly called out to her "brother." The robber fled.

"But Berta, your brudder is in Norway," Annie exclaimed.

"Ja, Annie, I know, but the robber didn't know."

Tonight Berta and Annie sang the old songs in the new land. Sophie Anderson joined the march and requested her favorite song, "Jesus may come today, Glad day! Glad day!" Beside her marched Eliza B. Henning Hommafos, the self-appointed poet laureate of Logan Square. Eliza was so fragile that she wore layers of clothes and piled her hair in soft puffs around her thin, artistic face. She had a poem for every occasion.

Emma Kjelsted limped with her cane. Happy Synove Knudsen, slender and regal in her latest Vogue fashion, marched with the handsome male newcomers. She was too independent to say yes to any of them. Gentle Lillie Olsen joined the Halbom sisters. Marching, singing . . . they were all there — the "Root" girls with their familiar Scandinavian names.

No one enjoyed the march more than Papa. He took turns with all the ladies and sang his heart out. These were his people! The red brick walls of the church on the square were not just walls of stone. They were walls built out of love — companionship for the lonely, comfort for those who were sorrowing and hope for those in despair. To the young, the walls contained the golden dreams of tomorrow and the moonlight and roses of romance.

No one walked alone! Together the young and the old dreamed the impossible dream — their heads held high. Their faith could bear the unbearable sorrow.

Papa's answer to death was God's answer: "I am the resurrection, and the life: he that believeth in Me, though he were dead, yet shall he live" (John 11:25). Papa believed that and shared that faith.

To those enduring the dark days of the great depression, Papa preached, "My God shall supply all your need according to His riches in glory by Christ Jesus" (Philippians 4:19).

To the lonely, Papa's confident voice rang out, "I will never leave thee, nor forsake thee" (Hebrews 13:5).

During difficult periods of change in a new land, Papa's answer came clear and strong from the Bible: "Jesus Christ, the same yesterday, and today, and forever" (Hebrews 13:8). "Forever, O LORD, Thy word is settled in heaven" (Psalm 119:89).

The candle in my hand flickered. I returned to the present as we stood for the closing benediction at the Myrtle Grove Presbyterian Church. Quietly we streamed out to our cars ready to return to the family time of Christmas Eve tradition. As we drove through the streets, we enjoyed the homes that had been beautifully decorated with lights. In the silence, I found myself remembering again that long ago "Root Fest."

The fest was over. The retreating steps of the "Root" girls could be heard in the snow as they wended their way to buses or elevated trains to return home. Papa quietly closed the door of Logan Square Church. As we walked home in the snow to our second-floor flat, Papa said, "Ja, ja, Margaret, there is nothing quite like the Root Fest!"

Perhaps tomorrow I'll tell the grandchildren all about it. But tonight we open our Christmas gifts.

Besides, it is time for a cup of coffee.

It was Christmas, 1985

9

Brooklyn, 1919

1919. IT WAS A LONG TIME AGO, yet I remember the setting.

Standing up in a crib behind a glass partition, I watched Papa's sad face. His black coat and scarf hung on his thin frame. He clutched his black hat in his hand, his face etched in grief. I reached out to touch him. "Hold me," I whimpered. He reached impulsively for me. But the glass partition kept us apart.

I remember standing alone in my long white gown, watching him wipe his eyes as he walked away.

The setting was the contagious ward in a New York City hospital where I was isolated in a glass cubicle, recovering from diphtheria.

Day after day, Papa came and stood behind the glass

partition, his strong, firm hands pressed against the window in a perpetual wave. Somehow, as young as I was, I understood I shouldn't cry.

Finally, the day came when the nurse dressed me in my own clothes. Then Papa wrapped me in a blanket and took me home on the streetcar to Grandmother's house. The wind was cold. My head hurt. I held my ears in pain. But I was going home!

With abandoned joy I kissed my sister Bernice. We clung to each other in a joyous reunion.

Bestemör Bertilda (Grandmother Bertilda) moved about her flat and cared for us all. Bernice and I played games, hiding in the velvet drapes that partitioned the living room from the kitchen.

Jule kakke lined the pantry shelves as Bestemör prepared for Christmas. The excitement in the air was not only for Christmas, but also for the new baby who was coming.

December 23, 1919, Grace was born — our Christmas angel. I helped Bestemör with the new baby, put cups on the table for coffee and made sure Papa had his sugar lumps.

When evening came, Bernice and I curled up together in our bed, secure in our family's love. We had Bestemör and a new baby. We had Mama and Papa. We were all together in Bestemör's Brooklyn flat.

I couldn't remember exactly how it happened, but we were in Woodville, Wisconsin, where Bernice and I were born, and then next we were on a long train ride. Then suddenly we were in Bestemör's flat in Brooklyn. If the memory were there at all, it was only a vague one — of Papa preaching and Mama burning her dress. I was too young to recognize Papa's sad, remorseful expression. Or to hear his strong, powerful voice grow hoarse. All I knew was that we were all together and Mama sang songs and told stories, and Bestemör took care of all of us. Papa didn't talk much. He slept in the daytime and went out to a watchman job at night. Mama still sang how